International Folktales
for English Language Learners

Published in 2012 by Global Awareness Publishing

Copyright © 2012 by Nancy Warnock Harmon

All rights reserved. No portion of this book may be reproduced, stored in a retrieval system, or transmitted in any form or by any means, mechanical, electronic, photocopying, recording or otherwise, without written permission from the publisher.

ISBN-13: 978-0-9822180-2-0

Illustrations, book and cover design by Daryl S. Fuller, Mountain Man Graphics.

The princpal text of this book was composed in Trebuchet MS.

The Center for Global Awareness

Albuquerque, New Mexico, USA

www.global-awareness.org

Acknowledgements

To my students in Thailand, Lebanon, and the US, thank you for sharing your stories with me and showing me how they can transform a classroom. To Steve Epstein, your wonderful book of Lao folktales has set a high standard and inspired me throughout the process of putting together this book. I am honored to include one of your tales. To Denise Ames, your patience and encouragement have been a steady influence throughout, and I am very grateful for your commitment to our work together at the Center for Global Awareness and your example of how to do it so well. To Daryl Fuller, your delightful drawings and design have turned the stories into a real book—thank you so much! To Ann Dempsey and Cathy House and their students, it was great fun to try the stories in your classrooms. I appreciate the opportunity and your feedback. And to my wonderful husband, Roger, my deep gratitude for all the many adventures and stories we have shared and for your unflagging faith in me as a writer.

Table of Contents

Notes to Teachers. 7

The Dog and the Meat. 13

The Boy Who Cried Wolf 17

The Tiger and the Mouse 23

The King and His Daughters 29

The Cobra. 35

The Walnut and the Pumpkin 42

The Sound of Money 45

Xieng Mieng Tricks the King 51

The Great Rain 57

La Llorona 65

Stone Soup 73

Notes to Teachers

How This Book Began

This collection of stories comes from my years of teaching English in a variety of places and to a diverse array of students. My very first teaching job was at an orphanage in the mountains above Beirut, Lebanon, where I am certain I learned more than the students. Just keeping order in a classroom of 50 students at the age of 22 was a full time job, not to mention creating materials with no library or copy machine. That is where I first began to recognize the importance of stories, especially folktales, in the English language classroom. The students delighted in telling me stories of the Middle Eastern trickster, Nasriddin. The telling evolved into writing and games inspired by the tales, activities that required no books or copies. The stories were fun and engaging and encouraged real communication.

More recently, I taught English at an organization called Empower in Bangkok, Thailand. The students, mostly women from Issan, the poorest but most soulful region of Thailand, had come to Bangkok to find work to help feed their families. They were at all levels of English language competence, and I had difficulty finding materials that were useful to all of them. Then my friend, Steve Epstein, gave me a copy of the book of Lao folktales he had compiled and translated while living and teaching in Laos. They were funny and clever, many of them about the Lao trickster, Xieng Mieng, so I decided to try one. The students' response astounded me. Because Issan is close to Laos, there's been an intertwining of cultures, and the students were very familiar with the stories of Xieng Mieng. They had grown up with these tales, and they were thrilled to see them translated into English with charming illustrations by a well-known Lao artist.

The students wanted more Xieng Mieng stories, so each week I copied one and brought it to class. Sometimes students who couldn't stay for the class came by just to pick up the story. Sometimes they would come to class and tell us about how they had told the story to an English-speaking boss, co-worker or friend. Shy, reticent students were more willing to speak in the classroom when talking about the story. When we ran out of Steve's stories, they told me other stories they had heard as children. We even wrote our own story. When we were using the tales, there was much laughter. Students told stories of their childhoods and family lore, memories inspired by the tales.

This experience convinced me of the power of folktales in the classroom. When I taught Mexican immigrants in Albuquerque, New Mexico, however, I was unable to find a compilation of folktales for use with beginning/intermediate students. (Since then I have found just one.) I began thinking about compiling a book myself—and here it is!

Using This Book

Because I've been a busy teacher myself for more than 30 years, I decided to include some exercises and activities with each of the stories to save teachers time. These include comprehension questions, new vocabulary words and practice, and language awareness (some might call it grammar) activities based on language used in each story. The use of these follow-up activities is purely optional, of course, and they will not fit every student or classroom; however, they may help teachers differentiate their instruction for varying ability levels and needs. Adult basic education students might just use the stories and vocabulary, while high school students might use the language awareness exercises.

I have sequenced the stories by increasing linguistic complexity. The first three stories are told with mostly simple and compound sentences in the present tense. Then there is a shift to past tense, while sentence structure is still quite simple. Gradually, sentence structure becomes more complex, and the language awareness exercises ask students to examine new structures, often through sentence combining. I have tried to repeat new vocabulary as often as possible. Students of any language must encounter a word at least six times before beginning to assimilate it into their own vocabulary, so repetition is essential. As a teacher, I would use these stories to break up the routine of workbooks and exercises from time to time, but they can be used as a unit for reading or cultural study.

Stories can provide the basis for a great variety of communicative activities that promote critical thinking and encourage skills used in other disciplines. Next you will find a list of such activities with a brief explanation. Many of the activities can be done in a group, which leads to spontaneous communication and cooperation.

Ideas for Activities with Folktales

- Have students draw a timeline of the story, illustrating each event with a small picture or symbol. This activity asks them to identify the main events of the story and determine chronological order.

- Present students with a series of pictures (stick drawings will do) and have students predict what the story is about.

- Understanding story schema is essential to reading comprehension. Introduce students to cause/effect and problem/solution schema. Ask students to analyze a story based on cause/effect or problem/solution schema.

- Present students with an empty Venn diagram. Have them compare two stories using the Venn diagram. Differences go on each side of the circle. Similarities go where the circles intersect in the middle.

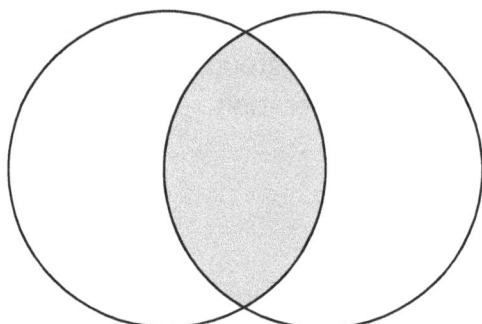

- Cut apart sentences from the story, mix them up and have students re-create the story in the proper order. Have them circle words that indicate order, such as then, later, finally.

- Crossword puzzles: Create crossword puzzles or word search puzzles with new vocabulary from the stories. Check the Internet for sites that create puzzles, sometimes free.

- Create a play or puppet show based on a story. This works particularly well with stories with a lot of dialog such as "Stone Soup" and " Xieng Mieng Tricks the King." Assign parts for different characters and choose a narrator to fill in the background.

- Have students create board games based on several stories. Bring in examples of different kinds of board games such as Chutes and Ladders and Monopoly. Have students make a colorful board with cards or spaces that provide setbacks and advantages to players.

- Cloze exercises: Re-print the story, leaving blank every four or five words. This is not a necessarily a vocabulary exercise. Leave out some of the building blocks of the sentence--prepositions, articles, verbs--to check not only for comprehension but for understanding of sentence construction.

- Create a cultural festival around each story. Bring in (or have students bring in) songs, poems, food and CDs from the region of origin of each story.

- Have students write brief story that illustrates a popular adage in their culture.

People acquire a new language more easily in an environment that is relaxed and natural. Through my years of teaching, I've found that folktales help to create that kind of atmosphere in the classroom—they can help reduce learner anxiety and encourage communication that is spontaneous and authentic. They make us laugh, remind us of our childhoods, exemplify how much people have in common, even if we come from different parts of the world, and return us to a simpler time in history, when our ancestors created these stories to entertain and to teach. I hope you and your students will enjoy these stories together as much as my students and I have.

This story is one of Aesop's fables. Aesop was a man from Greece who lived hundreds of years ago, but his stories have lived on and traveled all over the world. There is always a lesson to learn from one of Aesop's fables. Do you know any of these fables?

The Dog and the Meat

A hungry dog finds some fresh meat on the side of the road. She quickly picks up the meat in her mouth and looks for a place to eat. She walks across a low bridge and looks over the side. Below she sees another dog with a mouthful of meat. She wants that meat, too! She opens her mouth to grab the meat, but the meat falls out of her mouth and into the water. She is very surprised and walks away with no meat at all!

Questions to Talk About

What does the dog find?

What does she see in the water?

Why does she open her mouth?

What happens to the meat?

What can people learn from this story?

Using New Vocabulary

bridge—*noun:* Something that connects two sides of a river.

to grab—*verb:* to take something quickly and roughly.

surprised—*adjective:* a feeling when something unusual happens

Fill in the blanks from the story, using these words.

    mouth   hungry   meat   grab

surprised   bridge   no   looks   falls

A dog has some _____ in her mouth. She is _____ and wants to eat. She walks over a _____. She _____ over the side of the bridge. She sees a dog with meat in her _____. She opens her mouth to _____ the meat. Her meat _____ out. She is _____. She walks away with ____ meat.

Language Awareness

Highlight all the action words (verbs).

A dog finds some meat.

The dog walks over a bridge.

She looks over the side of the bridge.

She sees a dog below with meat.

The dog on the bridge wants more meat.

She opens her mouth.

The meat falls out of her mouth.

The dog walks away with no meat.

This is a very old and well-known story in America. Almost everyone can tell it. Have you ever heard this story in your country?

The Boy Who Cried Wolf

A boy named Daniel lives in a small village. He goes to the nearby hills everyday with his sheep. He stays with them all day and brings them home at night. He is alone all day with the sheep, so sometimes he feels bored.

One day Daniel is very bored. He climbs to the top of the hill and cries down to the village, "Help, help!! A wolf is attacking the sheep! Help me!"

The men in the village hear the cries. They run up the hill to help Daniel. They find him, but there is no wolf. "The wolf ran away," Daniel tells them. The men return to the village.

Several days later, Daniel feels a little lonely. He climbs to the top of the hill again. He cries, "Help, help. A wolf is attacking the sheep!"

Again the men run up the hill to help. Daniel tries hard not to smile. He tells them again, "The wolf ran away." The men return to the village.

A week later, Daniel sits with the sheep. He sees an animal running toward him. It is a wolf! The boy runs to the top of the hill and cries, "Help, help. A wolf is attacking the sheep! Please help me!"

The men from the village listen for a minute, but then they go back to work. The wolf kills two sheep, but Daniel can only watch. He is ashamed to return to the village that evening.

Questions to Talk About

Where does Daniel go every day?

Why does he feel bored?

What does he cry to the men?

How many times do the men try to help him?

Why do the men not come the last time he cries to them?

Sometimes you will hear that someone "cried wolf." What does it mean?

Using New Vocabulary

bored—*adjective*: feeling that nothing interesting is happening

to cry—*verb*: to call loudly in fear

to attack—*verb*: to try to hurt or kill an animal or person

lonely—*adjective*: alone

to kill—*verb*: to make something die

ashamed—*adjective*: feeling very guilty and embarrassed

Fill in the blanks with the following words.

hills	attacking	ashamed	kills
bored	return	wolf	help

A boy named Daniel takes his sheep to the _____ near his village. He is alone all day, so sometimes he feels _____. One day he cries, "Help, help, a wolf is _____ my sheep. Please help me!" The village men come running, but there is no wolf. The men _____ to the village. Daniel does this again. The men come running, but there is no _____. A week later, Daniel sees a wolf near the sheep. He calls for _____. No one comes. The wolf _____ two sheep. Daniel is _____ to return to the village.

Language Awareness

Ideas can be "glued together" or combined in English by using an assortment of "glue words." Some of the most common glue words are in the chart below: **and, but, or, so**. Each glue word shows a different relationship between the two ideas in a sentence. Study the chart below.

Glue Word	Meaning	Example
and	Adds information	He stays with the sheep all day, **and** he brings them home at night.
but	Shows a contrast between two ideas.	The men from the village listen for a minute, **but** then they go back to work.
so	Shows a result.	He is alone all day with the sheep, **so** sometimes he feels bored.
or	Provides a choice.	The men can run to help Daniel **or** they can go back to work.

Combine these sentences from the story into one sentence. Use the correct "glue word."

1. Daniel is alone all day with the sheep.
   He gets bored sometimes.

2. He cries to the men in the village.
   They run up the hill to help him.

3. There is no wolf.
   The men return to the village.

4. Daniel cries to the men again.
   They go back to work.

5. A wolf attacks the sheep.
   Daniel can only watch.

This is another one of Aesop's fables. What is the lesson in this fable? Do you know a story that teaches a similar lesson?

The Tiger and the Mouse

A tiny mouse walks through the jungle one day. She does not see a tiger, sleeping in front of her. She thinks the tiger is a large rock, so she walks over his shoulder. He wakes up angry.

"You wake me up, so now I will eat you for dinner!" he roars.

The mouse is very frightened of the tiger's huge teeth and long claws, but she says bravely, "Please let me live. If you let me live, one day I will do something good for you. I will pay you back. I promise I will."

The tiger laughs loudly. "What can such a small animal do for me, a huge tiger who is king of the jungle? That is very funny, my little mouse. Ha ha ha ha ha!!"

But the tiger is also amazed. He thinks, "How can a little mouse be so brave against a huge tiger?"

The tiger says, "You are very brave, little mouse. I am going to let you go this time, but do not bother me again, you silly thing. I never want to see you again! Go away!"

The mouse runs off into the jungle. She is very happy to be alive.

Months later, the little mouse is again walking through the forest. She hears a lot of noise up ahead, so she runs to see where it is coming from. Soon she sees the huge tiger. He is caught in a trap made of rope, and he is frightened. He cannot get his legs free. He roars and fights against the ropes.

The little mouse walks up to him and says, "Stop fighting, tiger. I can help you. Give me a few minutes, please."

The tiger is amazed to see the mouse again. "You silly mouse," he says. "How can you help the king of the forest? I will die in this trap."

"Be quiet. I will show you," says the mouse. The mouse begins to chew on the ropes. She chews and chews. Soon the ropes break! The tiger is free!

The tiger sees the chewed ropes, and he is surprised. He smiles and says, "Thank you, my little mouse friend! Never again will I laugh at the power of small creatures. We all have a place in the jungle."

Questions to Talk About

Where do the mouse and the tiger live?

Where does the mouse walk?

What catches the tiger?

How does the mouse help the tiger?

What does the tiger say to the mouse?

What is the lesson of this story?

Using New Vocabulary

amazed—*adjective*: surprised

to chew—*verb*: to break up food with the teeth

frightened—*adjective*: afraid

power—*noun*: strength

to pay back—*verb*: to return something

Fill in the blanks with the following words:

   chew   power   help   frightened
    promises   laughs   trap   noise
      surprised   fighting   free

A mouse walks over a tiger. The mouse is very _____of the tiger's huge teeth and claws, but she is very brave. She _____ the tiger she will help him later if he lets her live. The tiger _____, but he lets her go. She is happy to be alive. Months later, she hears a lot of _____ in the jungle. She finds the tiger caught in a rope _____. He is _____against the ropes. The mouse says, "Stop! I can _____you." She begins to _____on the ropes. Soon the ropes break and the tiger is _____. The tiger is _____. He says, "Thank you. Now I know that even small creatures have _____."

Language Awareness

Ideas can be "glued together" or combined in English by using an assortment of "glue words." Some of the most common glue words are in the chart below: **and, but, or, so**. Each glue word shows a different relationship between the two ideas in a sentence. Study the chart below.

Glue Word	Meaning	Example
and	Adds information	He is caught in a rope trap, **and** he is frightened.
but	Shows a contrast between two ideas.	The mouse is frightened, **but** she is also brave.
so	Shows a result.	She thinks the tiger is a rock, **so** she walks over his shoulder.
or	Provides a choice.	The mouse could run away, **or** she could help the tiger.

Find the glue words in the story. Which ideas do they tie together?

Combine the following sentences with one of the words above. Be careful not to repeat words in your sentence. Use pronouns instead of repeating nouns.

1. The mouse walks over the tiger.
   The tiger wakes up angry.

2. The tiger laughs at the mouse.
   The tiger lets her go free.

3. The mouse sees the tiger in a trap.
   The mouse goes to help him.

4. The mouse has sharp teeth.
   The mouse chews the ropes.

5. The tiger sees the chewed ropes.
   The tiger thanks the mouse for saving him.

Write five of your own sentences using the four glue words.

This folktale was told to a neighbor in California by her grandmother in Mexico when she was a child. She remembered it all her life and told it to me over tea one day.

The King Learns a Lesson

A king has three lovely daughters. They live happily as a family for many years. As the daughters get older, the king begins to wonder how much they really love him. The days pass, and he becomes more and more upset by this question.

One day he decides he must ask his daughters, so he calls them. "My dear daughters," he begins. "You are good and lovely daughters. I love you more than my own life, but I need to know just how much you love me."

The daughters are surprised at the question, but the first one thinks and then answers, "My dear father, I love you as much as all the shiny gold in the world!" The king smiles with happiness.

The second daughter then says, "Daddy dear, I love you as much as all the sparkling diamonds in the world." Again the king smiles happily at the answer.

The third daughter thinks a moment longer and says, "My sweet papa, I love you more than salt."

The king frowns and answers, "Daughter, I am disappointed with your answer. Salt is very ordinary and plain. My other two daughters love me more than you do!" He walks off angrily.

The third daughter is not upset. She runs to the kitchen and gives instructions to the palace cooks. The next day the family sits together at dinner. The king swallows a spoonful of soup, but he drops his spoon in surprise. "This soup has no flavor!" he cries. "Bring me the next course immediately!"

The servants bring more food. The king is hungry, so he takes a big bite of the enchiladas. Again he drops his fork and cries, "The enchiladas have no flavor! What has happened to my cooks? I cannot eat this food!"

The third daughter smiles and looks at her father. "My sweet papa," she says. "I have told the cooks to leave the salt out of the food so you will know how much I really love you!"

The king's frown becomes a smile. "Ah, my daughter, you are very clever, and you have taught your old father a very good lesson! The most valuable things in life are not always expensive!"

Questions to Talk About

What does the king wonder about his daughters?

Why is the king happy with the answers of the first two daughters?

Why is he unhappy with the third daughter's answer?

How does the third daughter explain her answer?

What does the king learn from his third daughter?

Vocabulary

to despair—*verb*: to feel hopeless; *noun*: a feeling of hopelessness

to wonder—*verb*: to question something

frown—*noun*: an expression of unhappiness on the face

sparkling—*adjective*: shining

disappointed—*adjective*: unhappy

flavor—*noun*: taste

surprise—*noun*: a feeling when something unexpected happens

valuable—*adjective*: important, dear

clever—*adjective*: smart

Use the words below to fill in the blanks.

sparkling   daughter   disappointed   wonders
valuable   flavor   angry   love

A king has three daughters. When they get older, he _____ how much they love him. He asks them to tell him. The first _____ loves him as much as shiny gold. The second daughter loves him as much as _____ diamonds. He is very happy. The third daughter loves him as much as salt. The king is very _____. The third daughter is not upset. She goes to the kitchen and speaks to the cooks. The next day the king is _____ because the food has no _____. The third daughter explains, "The food has no salt! Now you know how much I _____ you!" The king is no longer disappointed. His third daughter's answer teaches him a _____ lesson.

Language Awareness

Highlight *and, but* or, *so* in the story. Be sure to notice what ideas are tied together by these words.

Use *and, but* or, *so* to combine the following sentences. Do not repeat words. Use pronouns instead of nouns.

1. A king asks his daughters how much they love him.
   The daughters each tell the king.

2. The king is disappointed in his third daughter's answer.
   His daughter speaks to the cooks.

3. The king is hungry.
   The king cannot eat the food.

4. The cooks leave the salt out of the food.
   The food has no flavor.

5. The king learns a valuable lesson
   The king is happy with his daughter.

Folktales often include the animals that live among humans in different parts of the world. Cobras are common in Thailand. I heard this story from my students when I taught English in Thailand. They came from farming villages in northeast Thailand.

The Cobra

A farmer named Koong lives in Thailand. He is very sad and lonely because his wife has just died. He still walks to the rice paddies each day and works hard, but he returns to his small house sadly to eat his rice alone. He goes to bed early each night because there is nothing else to do.

One day as Koong walks home from the fields, he finds a small cobra on the path in front of him. The baby snake has a deep cut down its back. Because it is badly hurt, it doesn't try to run away from the farmer. He knows the tiny snake will die from its injury or be eaten by animals. He picks it up and gently carries it home in the palm of his hand.

Koong is happy with his new companion. Every day on his way home from the rice paddies, he looks for special insects for the cobra to eat. He puts fresh grass in its bed, and he talks to it every evening as he cooks his rice for dinner. He tells the cobra about his wife, his neighbors and his work. The young snake stretches out its head and looks at the farmer with its bright eyes. It seems to be listening.

The cobra grows healthy because Koong takes such good care of it. The cut on its back heals. Every day it gobbles the juicy insects the farmer brings. It sleeps lazily in the sun on the doorstep while the farmer is at work. At night, it curls up in its grassy bed. In a few weeks, it grows from a few inches long to more than a foot.

One day Koong comes home from work. As he enters his house and calls to his companion, the snake suddenly slides out from behind the door and bites the farmer on his leg. Koong cries out loudly in alarm. He falls to the floor in pain, holding his injured leg. "How can you bite me after all I did for you?" he shouts at the cobra.

The cobra holds its head high and looks at him with its bright eyes. As Koong gasps for breath, the cobra replies, "I bit you because I am a cobra."

Questions to Talk About

Why does the farmer feel so sad and lonely?

Why does the farmer take the cobra to his house?

How does the farmer feel about the snake?

Why is Koong surprised when the snake bites him?

Does the cobra's behavior make sense? Why or why not?

Do you think this story could have been written about a dog? A crocodile? An elephant? What is the difference between these animals?

Using New Vocabulary

rice paddies—*noun*: fields where farmers grow rice

weak -*adjective*: not strong

companion—*noun*: someone who is with you

injury—*noun*: a wound

gentle—*adverb*: not rough or harsh

to gobble—*verb*: to eat quickly

to heal—*verb*: to become healthy

alarm—*noun*: a sound of danger and fear

to gasp—*verb*: to breathe with difficulty

Put the following words in the appropriate blanks.

      gasps   heal   alarm   gobbles
          weak   injury   companion

Koong is sad and lonely because he has lost his wife. A baby cobra becomes his _____. The cobra is _____ because of an _____ on its back. Koong wants the injury to_____. The cobra _____ the insects Koong brings. It grows and grows. One day the cobra bites Koong. Koong shouts in _____ and _____ for breath.

Language Awareness

As you know, the words **and, but**, or, **so** are used to combine ideas together. They each show a different relationship between two ideas.

There are many other words that can also be used to combine ideas. **As** and **because** are two of these words.

Word	Meaning	Example
as	Shows that two ideas are happening at the same time.	As the farmer walks home from the rice paddies, he finds insects for the little cobra. or The farmer catches insects for the little cobra as he walks home from the rice paddies.
because	Shows that one idea caused another.	The cobra grows healthy because the farmer takes good care of it. or Because the farmer takes good care of it, the cobra grows healthy.

Highlight the sentences that use *as* and *because*. Notice the relationship between the two ideas as you read each sentence.

Now try it yourself. Combine these ideas, using one of the two words. Use pronouns in place of nouns so you don't repeat words in a sentence.

1. Koong walks home from the rice paddies
   Koong finds a small cobra on the path.

2. The cobra eats well.
   The cobra becomes healthy.

3. Koong has a new companion.
   Koong is not so lonely.

4. Koong talks to the cobra.
   The cobra seems to listen.

5. Koong falls to the floor.
   Koong shouts at the cobra.

Now write five of your own sentences about your daily life using *as* and *because*.

Nasriddin stories are popular in Turkey and much of the Muslim world. Nasriddin may have been a real person, a religious leader who lived hundreds of years ago. His stories are still told today, and I heard many of them when I taught English in Lebanon in a small school in the mountains. Here are two of those stories.

The Pumpkin and the Walnut.

One hot afternoon, Nasriddin lay in the shade of a great walnut tree, feeling very sleepy. He looked up into the branches of the huge tree and noticed the small nuts hanging from the branches.

He thought to himself, "It is strange that Allah put such small nuts on the branches of such a large tree. I think it would make more sense for the walnut tree to bear pumpkins and the fragile vines of the pumpkin to bear walnuts instead."

With that thought, he fell asleep in the cool shade of the giant tree. Several hours later, he awoke suddenly when something hit him on the head. Rubbing his head, he looked around and noticed a walnut lying on the grass near his head.

"Praise be to Allah!" he cried. "Now I understand why the walnut tree does not bear pumpkins!"

Questions to Talk About

Why does Nasriddin think pumpkins should grow on a large tree?

Why does he change his mind?

Do you sometimes wonder why things are the way they are? Give an example.

Using New Vocabulary

instead—*adverb*: in place of

to notice—*verb*: to see

to bear—*verb*: to carry, to grow

nap—*noun*: a short sleep

to make sense—*verb*: to be reasonable

fragile—*adjective*: easily hurt

vines—*noun*: plants that grow along the ground

Allah—*noun*: name for God in Muslim religion

Fill in the blanks with the following words. You will not need one of the words.

    instead   vine   sense   noticed   bear
              pumpkins   nap   hit

Nasriddin was taking a _____ under a large walnut tree. He thought the large tree should _____ pumpkins. The fragile _____ of the pumpkin should bear walnuts. That would make more _____. He fell asleep under the tree. Later he woke up when something _____ him on the head. He looked around and _____ the small walnut on the ground. Then he knew why the tree did not bear pumpkins _____ of walnuts.

The Smell of Soup and the Sound of Money

One day a hungry beggar stopped by an inn to ask for food. The innkeeper gave the beggar a piece of bread and sent him away. Hoping to find more food, the beggar stopped by the kitchen of the inn. He smelled the fragrance of soup coming from the stove and took a deep breath. Just then, the innkeeper walked in the door. He was angry, and he said to the beggar, "You must pay if you take more food! I cannot give you more."

"But I only smelled the soup. I did not eat it," replied the beggar.

"Then you must pay for the smell of the soup!" answered the innkeeper.

"But no one pays for the fragrance of a flower or rain in the wind! I will not pay for the smell of your soup!" shouted the beggar.

They argued and argued but found no solution. Finally they took the problem to the mosque to find Nasriddin. They explained the problem.

Nasriddin listened and then said to the innkeeper, "So you want the beggar to pay you for the smell of the soup? I will pay you instead!"

Taking two coins out of his pocket, he dropped them together so they clinked. "There," he said to the innkeeper. "You have now been paid for the smell of soup with the sound of money. Go on your way and do not bother me again with such ridiculous matters."

Questions To Talk About

Why did the beggar stop by the inn?

Why did he go to the kitchen?

Why did the innkeeper want money?

What was Nasriddin's solution to the problem?

Write a moral this story.

Using New Vocabulary

beggar—*noun*: a person who asks others for food or money (begs)

inn—*noun*: hotel

innkeeper—*noun*: person in charge of the inn

fragrance—*noun*: a good smell

to argue—*verb*: to disagree with words

solution—*noun*: the answer to a problem

clink—*noun*: the sound of metal on metal

ridiculous—adjective: silly, unreasonable

mosque—noun: place of worship in Muslim religion

Fill in the blanks with the words above. You will *not* use one of the words, and one word will be used twice.

fragrance argued solution sound
beggar ridiculous smell

A hungry _____ stopped at an inn to ask for food. The innkeeper gave him some bread. The beggar went to the kitchen to look for more food. He smelled the _____ of the soup. The innkeeper found him there. He wanted money for the _____ of the soup. He and the beggar _____ a long time, but they found no _____ to the problem. They went to see Nasriddin at the mosque. His _____ to the problem was to pay for the smell of soup with the _____ of the coins.

Language Awareness

Many ideas in English are combined in sentences with words that act like glue to keep the two ideas together such as **and, but, or, so**. Sentences can also be combined by creating a phrase that begins with **a verb + ing**. Look at the example.

Sentence 1	Sentence 2	Verb	Combination
Nasriddin lay on the ground under a walnut tree.	He felt very sleepy on a hot afternoon.	Feel + ing	Feeling very sleepy on a hot afternoon, Nasriddin lay on the ground under a walnut tree.
The beggar stopped by the kitchen of the inn.	He hoped to find more food.	Hope + ing	Hoping to find more food, the beggar stopped by the kitchen of the inn.

Highlight the sentences in the story with this kind of combination.

Now try it yourself. Be sure the verb phrase is next to the word it describes.

1. Nasriddin looked up at the tree. (use look+ing)
   He noticed small nuts on the branches.

2. He felt sleepy. (use feel + ing)
   Nasriddin took a nap under the tree.

3. He woke up suddenly. (use wake + ing)
   He noticed the small nut on the grass.

4. The beggar went to the kitchen. (use look + ing)
   He looked for more food.

5. They found no solution to their argument.
   (use find + ing)
   They took their problem to the mosque.

Now write five of your own sentences using this structure.

Xieng Mieng appears in many stories from Laos and Northern Thailand. He is very clever, so clever that he can even trick the king! My students in Bangkok came from Northern Thailand to find jobs in the city, and they loved to read and share these stories that they grew up with. I want to thank Steve Epstein, a dear friend and fellow teacher who collected and translated these stories, for his permission to use this story in the book.

The King Tries to Trick Xieng Mieng

The weather in the kingdom was lovely. The sky was bright blue, and cool breezes played with the fluffy clouds.

"Xieng Mieng," said the king, "the weather is perfect for a picnic in the countryside. We will go to the pond near the forest. "

"How will we get there?" asked Xieng Mieng, though he already knew the answer.

"I, being the king, will ride on my beautiful white horse and you, being Xieng Mieng, will walk."

"Of course, Your Majesty."

The king and Xieng Meing ate the picnic lunch prepared by the royal chefs. There was papaya salad and barbecued chicken and sticky rice. For dessert they ate mangoes. The horse ate some grass.

"Xieng Mieng," said the king, "you are a clever man. It is true that you have tricked me a few times. Now I challenge you to trick me again. I challenge you to trick me so that I will go into the pond. If you can trick me into going into the pond, I will let you ride my horse back home."

"Your Majesty, you are much cleverer than I. You know I cannot trick you into going into the pond."

"So, Xieng Mieng, you admit that I am cleverer than you."

"Of course, Your Majesty, you are cleverer than me. But, Your Majesty, if you go into the pond, I can trick you into coming out of the pond."

"Hah! Let me see you try! I accept your challenge."

And the king walked into the pond.

"I am cleverer than you, Xieng Mieng," laughed the king as he stood in the middle of the pond.

Xieng Mieng sat down on the grass and finished up the rest of the mangoes.

"Xieng Mieng, here I am. I am in the pond . Now you try to trick me to come out of the pond."

Xieng Mieng yawned and lay down on the grass and took a nap.

"Xieng Mieng, here I am. I am in the pond. Now trick me into coming out of the pond!"

Xieng Mieng woke up from his sleep. He yawned and stretched.

"It is getting late, Your Majesty. I must go back now. I cannot trick you to come out of the pond. Since you will be staying in the pond, you will not have any need for your horse. So I know it won't be a problem if I ride it back."

Xieng Mieng mounted the king's beautiful white horse.

"Wait! You tricked me again! Wait!" said the king as he watched a laughing Xieng Mieng go galloping away.

Questions to Talk About

Why does the king want to go on a picnic?

How do they travel to the pond?

What does the king want Xieng Mieng to do?

What is Xieng Mieng's challenge?

How does Xieng Mieng win?

How clever is the king?

Using New Vocabulary

picnic—*noun*: a meal outdoors

clever—*adjective*: smart

trick—*noun*: a joke to show you are clever. *verb*: to make someone do something they don't want to do

challenge—*noun*: a task that is very difficult. *verb*: to ask someone to do something difficult

pond—*noun*: a small lake

to gallop—*verb*: the way a horse runs fast

nap—*noun*: a short sleep during the day

to mount—*verb*: to climb up on something

Fill in the blanks with the following words. You will not use one of the words.

galloped   trick   nap   picnic   pond
challenged   yawned   cleverer   out

Xieng Mieng and the king went on a _____.
They sat beside a _____ to eat their lunch.
The king _____ Xieng Meing to trick him into going into the pond. Xieng Mieng said he can only _____ him to come out of the pond. The king walked into the pond and told Xieng Mieng he was ready for the trick. Xieng Mieng _____ and lay down for a _____. The king called again. Xieng Mieng woke up and said he could not trick the king to get _____.   He took the king's horse and _____ home. The king was tricked again!

Language Awareness

Look carefully at the punctuation in this story. When you write the exact words of a speaker, you need to use quotation marks (") at the beginning and end of the quote ("_____"). You also need to begin a new paragraph when there is a new speaker. What other punctuation do you see with quotation marks in this story?

Change the following sentences into quotations, using all the correct punctuation.

1. The king said Xieng Mieng, let's go on a picnic.
2. The king said Xieng Mieng, you must walk beside my horse.
3. The king said Xieng Mieng, you are more clever than me.
4. Xieng Mieng said to the king I cannot trick you to go into the pond.
5. Xieng Mieng said to the king now I will ride your horse home.

Now write five sentences using quotation marks.

Native American people in the United States have a strong tradition of storytelling. These people have lived and often still live close to the earth, aware and respectful of nature around them. Their stories explain how the world was created and how people came to be in it, and they explain things about the creatures and the environment around them.
I heard this story when I taught English on the Navajo reservation in New Mexico.

The Great Rain

A Legend from Native America

One summer in North America, the weather became very dark and cloudy, thunder crashed in the sky above, and the wind howled. Nokomis, the great spirit of the earth, was worried. It was the **wildest** storm she had ever seen. She called to Thunderbird, the spirit of the sky, "Why is the sky so dark and stormy?" she asked.

Thunderbird answered, "Because I am jealous! The people love you **more** than they love me! I am going to send rain and wind to show the people my power. It will rain and rain and rain. The rain will wash away the animals, rivers, fields and people. Then they will understand that I am powerful."

Nokomis was frightened. She decided that she must warn the people to prepare for a flood. She turned herself into an old woman, and she walked from village to village. "The rains are coming. You must move to **higher** ground! Please hurry. You will not be safe if you stay here! You will drown!" she shouted.

Most people listened and were frightened. They packed up their clothing, food and cooking pots and left with their families. They hurried up to the hills where they could be **safer**. But in the last village, the people were dancing. They sang and danced around a fire and shook their rattles as they danced.

They laughed at the old woman when they heard her warning.

"What can this old woman know?" they asked each other. "We must continue our celebration!" And they continued to dance around the fire, shaking their rattles.

Nokomis was very angry. "These people are very foolish," she thought. "I could let them drown, but I will teach them a lesson instead."

Suddenly, the dancers saw with surprise that they were becoming **smaller and thinner.** They lost their arms and legs, and soon they were sliding along the ground. Their rattles appeared at the end of their long thin bodies. They hid under rocks away from the storm.

Sometimes when you are walking in the desert on a warm day, you might meet some of these creatures. They will rise up and sway back and forth as they did when they danced around the fire. And they will rattle their tails. They want to warn you to run away, just as the old woman tried to warn them.

Questions to Talk About

Why did Thunderbird send a terrible storm?

Who went to warn the people about the storm?

Why did Nokomis become angry with the people in the last village?

Why didn't Nokomis let the dancers drown?

What happened to the dancers?

Are there stories in your culture that explain how things came to be? Give some examples. Why do you think people create stories like these?

Vocabulary

thunder—*noun*: loud sound in the sky during a storm

to howl—*verb*: to make a frightening sound

frightened—*adjective*: afraid

jealous—*adjective*: wanting what someone else has

to prepare—*verb*: to make ready

flood—*noun*: a huge amount of water

to warn—*verb*: to speak about danger coming

rattle—*noun*: something you can shake to make a sound. *verb*: to make a sound with a rattle

to slide—*verb*: to move smoothly along the ground

creatures—*noun*: animals

power—*noun*: strength

Fill in the blanks with the following words. You will use one word twice.

slide   warn   jealous   prepare
frightened   thunder   creatures   power

One summer in North America, there was a terrible storm. Thunderbird, the spirit of the sky, was _____ of Nokomis, the spirit of the earth. He wanted to show his _____ with a huge storm. Nokomis ran through villages to _____ the people to _____ for a flood. Rain began to fall and _____ roared above. The people were _____. They packed their things and ran to the hills. One village did not run because they were dancing. Nokomis changed them to long, thin _____ that could _____ along the ground. Sometimes you might see these creatures while you are walking. They will rise up and rattle their tails to _____ you to run away from them.

Language Awareness

Use "er" or "more" to compare two things.	Use "est" or "most" to compare three or more things
They hurried to the hills where they could be **safer.** You must move to **higher** ground! The people love you **more than** they love me!	June 21 is the **longest** day of the year. My mother is the **happiest** woman I know. The people love you **most** of all.
Use "more" for long words. The black cat is **more beautiful than** the white one.	Use "most" for long words. The black cat is **the most beautiful of all the cats.**

Fill in the blank with the correct word.

1. The people moved up to _____ and _____ ground. (high, safe)
2. It was the _____ storm she had ever seen. (wild)
3. This is the _____ colorful of the three dresses. (more or most)
4. It was the _____ thunder they had ever heard. (loud)
5. The king is _____ powerful than the farmer. (more or most)
6. My wedding was the _____ day of my life. (happy)
7. My sister Julie is _____ than my sister Margie. (tall)
8. Margie is the _____ of the two sisters. (short)

Now write five of your own sentences comparing two or more things.

I have lived in New Mexico for many years. This story is a favorite of people who live along the Rio Grande, both in Mexico and New Mexico. Everyone knows it. There are different ways to tell this story. Here is one version.

La Llorona
The Weeping Woman

Once upon a time, there was a lovely young woman named Maria who lived in a small village along the Rio Grande River. She had hair as black as raven feathers, eyes that shone in the moonlight and a smile that lit up her face. She loved to laugh, and she played the guitar with great skill. Many men wanted to marry her **when** she got older, but she was very proud. She didn't feel any of them were good enough for her. She refused them all and continued to wait for the perfect man.

One day a very handsome man came to town. He sat straight and tall on a spirited horse. His hair was as black as coal, and his eyes flashed when he looked at women. His laughter echoed through the streets at night **when** he had been drinking. Maria fell instantly in love with this man called Ricardo. **When** Ricardo saw Maria, it was love at first sight for him, too. Maria's parents didn't like this wild new man in town, so the two young people met secretly. Their love grew stronger, and finally they ran away to get married.

They lived happily in love. They laughed, sang with Maria's guitar and enjoyed life together on the banks of the Rio Grande. They had two sweet children— Manuel and Rosa. After several years, however, Ricardo began to travel, and he stayed away for weeks at a time. **When** he returned, he brought gifts to the children, but he barely spoke to Maria. **When** he was home, he played and talked with the children but ignored her. This went on for months. Proud Maria's jealousy and anger grew with each night she spent alone.

One terrible day **when** Maria was walking with Manuel and Rosa, she saw Ricardo come into town with a young and beautiful woman in his carriage. He jumped down to hug the children but didn't even look at Maria. He returned to the carriage and drove off with the young woman.

Maria went crazy with jealousy and despair. As she and the children reached the river, she suddenly pushed both children into the rushing water below. They shouted for help, but the sound of the water covered their cries. Soon they sank and disappeared.

Maria was instantly horrified at what she had done! She looked into the river and screamed in despair, "My

children, my children!" Overcome by grief and guilt, she jumped off the bank and into the water.

Maria lived many years ago, but people who live along the Rio Grande today say that her ghost still haunts the banks of the river. At night **when** the wind blows, they can hear her mournful cries as she searches for her children. Parents warn children not to stay near the river too late because they might feel the icy breath and bony fingers of La Llorona, the Weeping Woman, who wanders hopelessly and forever, never able to rest in peace.

Questions to Talk About

Why did Maria not want to marry the men of her village?

Why did Maria and Ricardo run away to get married?

Why did Maria think Ricardo was losing interest in her?

Why was Maria jealous of her children?

Why did Maria throw herself into the river?

Are there stories of ghosts in your country? Tell a story to the class.

Why do you think people tell ghost stories?

Using New Vocabulary

carriage—*noun*: a vehicle pulled by horses

to ignore—*verb*: to pay no attention to something

overcome—*adjective*: unable to resist

guilt—*adjective*: a feeling of responsibility for doing something wrong

grief—*noun*: extreme sadness

to wander—*verb*: to move around with no specific destination

mournful—*adjective*: sad about the death of someone

weeping—*adjective* or *verb*: crying

horrified—*adjective*: feeling horror

to haunt—*verb*: to come as a ghost

ghost—*noun*: spirit of a dead person

Fill in the blanks below with one of the words below. You will not use one of the words.

ghost guilt wanders despair carriage
jealous married horrified attention

Maria and Ricardo ran away to get _____, and they lived happily for a few years with their two children. Then Ricardo began to stay away from his family. He paid _____ to the children but not to Maria. Maria was very _____. One day she saw him in a _____ with another woman. Filled with _____, she pushed her children into the Rio Grande River. She was immediately _____, so she threw herself into the river, too. Today people hear the cries of her _____ . She _____ on the banks of the river, calling to her children.

Language awareness

The word **when** can be a glue word like **and, but, or, so.** It shows a time relationship between two ideas. Notice the two ideas in the sentences with **when** highlighted in the story.

Glue Word	Meaning and Use	Example
when	Used when two events depend on one another and happen nearly at the same time (although one event usually happens a little before the other event).	When he returned, he brought presents to the children. or He brought presents to the children when he returned.

Combine the following sentences using *when*. One event happens a little before the other and needs the *when*. Put a comma after the *when* phrase if it is at the beginning of the sentence. Try to use both ways of writing the sentence.

1. Maria met Ricardo.
   She knew he was the man for her.

2. Ricardo saw Maria.
   It was love at first sight.

3. Ricardo ignored Maria.
   He returned from his travels.

4. Maria saw Ricardo with another woman
   She felt very jealous.

5. Maria jumped into the river.
   She realized what she had done to her children.

Write five of your own sentences using *when*.

This is a story that I first heard as a young child. I have never forgotten it, so I am including it for you to enjoy. I believe it originally came from Eastern Europe.

Stone Soup

Once upon a time, a soldier was traveling home from a terrible war. He had traveled many days, and he was weak with hunger. He thought, "I cannot go further without food. I will ask the people in this village to give me something to eat. I am wearing a uniform, and I fought to make them safe from the enemy. They will be generous with me."

He knocked on the door to a small, wooden house on the corner. An old man with white hair answered.

"Please, do you have food to share with a hungry soldier? I will take anything you have," said the soldier. The old man replied, "The war has left me with nothing, sir. I have nothing to share." And he closed the door with a bang.

The soldier went to the next house. A baby cried inside. He knocked on the door, and a young woman with a baby in her arms answered. "Please, do you have food to share with a hungry soldier?" he asked again.

The woman replied, "I have four children, and they do not have enough to eat. I cannot help you." She shut the door.

He went to four more houses to ask for food, but he got the same answer each time. No one had food to share. He was very disappointed and even hungrier, so he sat down on a pile of stones to rest. Suddenly he had an idea. He saw a young boy on a bicycle, and he said to the boy, "I want to make some soup for the whole village. Can you bring me a large kettle and spoon from your house? Tell everyone along the way that there will be free soup in the park very soon."

The boy rode off and soon returned with a large black kettle and spoon. A crowd began to gather as people heard about free soup. The soldier built a fire on the side of the road and set the kettle on top of it. He looked up at them and said, "I'm going to make you a delicious soup from the stones lying here. I learned how do to this while traveling as a soldier. People everywhere eat stone soup!"

"How can you make soup from stones?" a man shouted. "I don't believe it!"

"I will show you.," answered the soldier. "But first, a few extra things will make it

74

more tasty. Does anyone have onions growing in their garden?"

The woman with the baby ran off to bring the onions. When she returned, the soldier sliced them and dropped them into the boiling water in the kettle. "Now do you add the stones?" asked the boy on the bike.

"Not yet. I will also need some tomatoes to make it really delicious," said the soldier. An old man limped away to bring tomatoes from his garden. When he returned, the soldier chopped them and put them in the soup. The boy on the bike asked again, "Now do we put in the stones?"

Again the soldier answered, "Not yet. The soup will be so much better with some herbs and a little garlic. Can anyone bring me garlic and herbs and a spoonful of salt?" Several more people ran to their gardens and returned with salt, herbs, garlic. A grandmother crossed the street and returned with green beans and zucchini. The soldier dropped them in and stirred the soup, and the villagers smelled its fragrance.

The boy asked again, "Now do we put in the stones? The soldier answered once more, "Not yet. To finish this wonderful soup, it would be nice to have some bones or leftover meat scraps." The village butcher ran to his shop and returned with a bag of bones and pieces of beef and chicken. The soldier added them and stirred the soup. It was even more fragrant and made the villagers very hungry. Finally, the soldier called, "The soup is ready! Go home and get bowls and spoons, and we will eat this delicious soup together!"

The villagers all ran home and returned with bowls and spoons. Some even brought loaves of bread and pieces of cheese. Others brought musical instruments. The soldier served each person as much as he or she could eat. After they ate, they played music, danced and told stories.

Suddenly the boy with the bike jumped up and shouted, "But he never put the stones in the soup!"

The soldier answered, "That's right, young man. And I am going to leave the stones here in the village so you

will remember that great things happen when many people work together with generous spirits! Thank you all for your generosity. You each helped to create this delicious soup and happy evening."

Questions to Talk About

Why did the soldier think people would give him food?

Why did the people bring food for the soup?

Why did the soldier not use the stones?

Why did the soldier want to leave the pile of stones where it was?

Using New Vocabulary

uniform—*noun*: clothing worn by soldiers and police

crowd—*noun*: a large group of people

to share—*verb*: to divide and give something to another person

generous—*adjective*: giving freely

fragrance—*noun*: a good smell

enemy—*noun*: a person who is against you

scraps—*noun*: small pieces of something like food or cloth.

Put the following words in the blanks. You will not use one word.

enemy   uniform   fragrant   crowd
disappointed   share   generous

A soldier in a _____ was coming home from the war. He asked people in a village to _____ some food with him. He was _____ because no one had food to share. He decided to make soup from stones. A _____ gathered to watch. Some people brought vegetables for the soup. It began to smell _____. Everyone enjoyed the soup made by the _____ villagers.

Language Awareness

Words in English can be changed a little to play different roles in a sentence. You can increase your vocabulary more quickly if you watch for words like this. Look at the examples from the story.

Word	Noun	Adjective
fragrant, fragrance	The villagers smelled the fragrance of the soup.	The soup was fragrant.
hungry, hunger	The soldier was weak with hunger.	The soldier was very hungry.
generosity, generous	The soldier thanked the villagers for their generosity.	The generous people were happy with the soup.

Fill in the blanks using the words in the chart.

1. The _____ soup made them hungry (fragrant, fragrance).
2. The _____ of the soup made them hungry. (fragrant, fragrance)
3. Great _____ made the soldier ask for food. (hungry, hunger)
4. The _____ soldier asked for food in the village. (hungry, hunger)
5. The _____ of the villagers made the soup. (generous, generosity)
6. The _____ villagers made the soup. (generous, generosity)

Be sure to watch for these kinds of words. You will find them everywhere. Keep a list! Start with words from these stories such as **warn and warning, power and powerful.**

81

www.ingramcontent.com/pod-product-compliance
Lightning Source LLC
Chambersburg PA
CBHW061504040426
42450CB00008B/1480